Neerajkumar Maurya
Shristi Maurya

An Efficient Algorithm For Shortest Path Tree In Dynamic Graph

Neerajkumar Maurya
Shristi Maurya

An Efficient Algorithm For Shortest Path Tree In Dynamic Graph

LAP LAMBERT Academic Publishing

Impressum / Imprint

Bibliografische Information der Deutschen Nationalbibliothek: Die Deutsche Nationalbibliothek verzeichnet diese Publikation in der Deutschen Nationalbibliografie; detaillierte bibliografische Daten sind im Internet über http://dnb.d-nb.de abrufbar.
Alle in diesem Buch genannten Marken und Produktnamen unterliegen warenzeichen-, marken- oder patentrechtlichem Schutz bzw. sind Warenzeichen oder eingetragene Warenzeichen der jeweiligen Inhaber. Die Wiedergabe von Marken, Produktnamen, Gebrauchsnamen, Handelsnamen, Warenbezeichnungen u.s.w. in diesem Werk berechtigt auch ohne besondere Kennzeichnung nicht zu der Annahme, dass solche Namen im Sinne der Warenzeichen- und Markenschutzgesetzgebung als frei zu betrachten wären und daher von jedermann benutzt werden dürften.

Bibliographic information published by the Deutsche Nationalbibliothek: The Deutsche Nationalbibliothek lists this publication in the Deutsche Nationalbibliografie; detailed bibliographic data are available in the Internet at http://dnb.d-nb.de.
Any brand names and product names mentioned in this book are subject to trademark, brand or patent protection and are trademarks or registered trademarks of their respective holders. The use of brand names, product names, common names, trade names, product descriptions etc. even without a particular marking in this works is in no way to be construed to mean that such names may be regarded as unrestricted in respect of trademark and brand protection legislation and could thus be used by anyone.

Coverbild / Cover image: www.ingimage.com

Verlag / Publisher:
LAP LAMBERT Academic Publishing
ist ein Imprint der / is a trademark of
OmniScriptum GmbH & Co. KG
Heinrich-Böcking-Str. 6-8, 66121 Saarbrücken, Deutschland / Germany
Email: info@lap-publishing.com

Herstellung: siehe letzte Seite /
Printed at: see last page
ISBN: 978-3-659-31013-3

Abstract

Graph theory is the study of graph, in which any model is represented pairwise with some relation. By using these graphs many problems from the different fields of engineering can be solved easily. In most of the fields graphs are used and, their one has to find shortest path tree. But because of a big graph, time is major concern and to minimize that one algorithm has been proposed in this thesis.

This thesis proposes an efficient technique for computing Shortest Path Tree (SPT) in the dynamic graph, where the weights of edges changes frequently. Algorithm minimizes the time complexity of the computation for SPT. This computation shows that algorithm works properly for the fully Dynamic Graph also, with multiple weight change. The proposed algorithm traverses only that part of the graph, which is likely to be affected from the weight changes. Since the affected part of the tree may contain zero number of nodes, in that case no time is required for the updated SPT. In other cases where some nodes are there then the complexity can be shown asymptotically with Big-O notation.

If the graph is static i.e. not changing its weight then SPT is being calculated once and that remains same forever. If graph is dynamic i.e. changing its weight then proposed technique finds new SPT with traversing minimum number of vertices. This technique extends a few state-of-art dynamic SPT algorithms to handle multiple edge weight updates, and find the SPT. A function based on the location of current node/ state is used to vary the cost of the goal node and the search is done with minimum state space and exploring only affected nodes, by using this approaches problem is solved in minimum time.

In this thesis, artificial dataset has been used to compare the results and to show the correctness of the algorithm. The complexity of the proposed algorithm has been compared with well-known Dijkstra's SPT algorithm. Dijkstra's algorithm is having the complexity in order of $O(N^2)$ if that is implemented in simple priority queue. Here this proposed algorithm is also implemented in simple priority queue, and it is having different complexity for different cases. Algorithm's complexity is $O(bd)$ in worst case, $O(E)$ in average case, and $O(1)$ in best case. Here asymptotic notation has been used since time varies cases to cases and machine to machine. In complexity b, d, E and N stands for branching factor, depth of affected sub-tree number of edges and number of nodes respectively. The performance of the algorithm is measured on the basis of graph size, number of changed edges(NCE).

By considering above conditions proposed algorithm shows a high time difference to compute SPT in any dynamic graph. And this time reduction is upto even 100% in some cases, and on an average time reduction is about 80%, if compared with the Dijkstra's SPT algorithm.

Acknowledgements

A journey is easier when you travel together. Interdependence is certainly more valuable than independence. It is a pleasant aspect that I have now the opportunity to express my gratitude for all of those who helped me to carry out this work.

I begin with thanking God for helping me in situations when I needed him the most. I would like to thank to my parents and family. I am grateful to Dr. Kamal Shah (Dean R & D and H.O.D. I.T. Department), Dr. Vinayak A. Bharadi (Dy. H.O.D. I.T. Department for their valuable comments that have improved quality of this work.

I am grateful to my younger sister Shristi Maurya, who helped me a lot for completion of this thesis and implementation of the algorithm.

The chain of my gratitude would be definitely incomplete if I would forget to thank the first cause of this chain, my deepest and sincere gratitude to my family members and friends for inspiring and guiding throughout my dissertation work.

Neeraj Kumar Maurya

List of Contents

List of Figures

List of Tables

Abbreviations and Symbols

G   Graph
E   Edges
V   Vertices
N   Number of vertices
C   Cost of path
W   Weight of edge
SPT   Shortest Path Tree
DSPT   Dijkstra's Shortest Path Tree
b   Branching factor
d   Depth

Chapter 1. **Introduction**

1.1 Background

The Graph is the set of Edges and Vertices i.e. G=(V, E, W). Where V shows the vertices and E shows the Edges, W is the weight assigned to edge. And there may be any combination of vertices which can be shown with the help of edges. And these edges may be directed or undirected depends on the property of graph. If graph can be traversed in only one direction by using any edge then that is known is directed edge, and if travelling is irrespective of direction of the edge then that is known as undirected graph. Edges may have their weights, it may be assigned based on the distance or any other transition factor which can delay the transition. If weights are assigned to the edges then that is known as weighted graph, otherwise graph is known as non-weighted graph where the weight of each edge is considered to be unit.

Graph is being used in a wide area for computation in so many field including, computer networking, Electrical networking, project management, circuit designing, GPS to find paths etc. The common task which is done in almost all the applications is finding path from any node known as source to other node known as destination. While finding the path system has to maintain the minimum cost throughout the process so that it should take minimum time to accomplish any task. The main problem is to compute shortest path tree with algorithm having minimum complexity. Some algorithms are being used in real world like, Dijkstra's Shortest Path Tree(DSPT).

The Dijkstra's algorithm which is mentioned in the previous paragraph is working excellently with Static Graph(Static Graph is the graph in which the weight of the edges remain same or constant always). In case if the weight of the graph changes then these algorithm will have to recomputed SPT again starting from source and it will take same time as computing the SPT for that graph first time.

1.2 Motivation

Now a days the Graph theory is widely used in almost all the fields, especially in networking, database management, biotechnologies and so many others. The main purpose of the graph in this is to do any computation fast and efficiently and to retrieve any data with less time complexity. Since space complexity is also an issue but it is very cheap, and easily available. So the main focus is to reduce the time complexity.

If any dataset is assumed in which one has to store and retrieve any information with some conditions, like having longest sequence of some combination, for example in D.N.A. there are nucleobases (G,A,T,C) attached to the sugar. To match the D.N.A. samples one has to check the longest sequence of nucleobase combination. If any one of them is changing its property it will have to check that from starting and that is time consuming.

In networking field, data packets has to be transferred from source location to destination with minimum time for that system has to calculate minimum number of nodes in its way so that time will be reduced. But in this there are so many other obligations like traffic, which is dynamic in nature and varies time to time continuously, which may also affect the speed of data transmission. In this scenario if route have been calculated from the source to destination with minimum cost, its not necessary that that would be persistent. If any node is broken down or traffic is exceeded then system will have to find other alternative route and fro that it will compute that path again from source to destination. But if routes are being recomputed from starting then it will again have same amount of time as the path was never searched before.

From above scenario underlined idea is to compute that path only which will be affected from those changes, it will definitely reduce the time on a big scale.

1.3 Objectives

The main objective of this work is to propose an algorithm which will find shortest path tree in a given dynamic graph. Here dynamic graph means the weighted directed which may change its weight any time. And this work will process only that part of the tree which will be affected from those changes.

And by applying this, proposed algorithm has to reduce the time complexity for searching SPT in the dynamic graph after getting some changes in any combination of edges (links), whether the traffic is increasing, decreasing. Any such type of event will trigger this algorithm to compute SPT but with only affected part of the graph.

1.4 Layout of Thesis

In proposed algorithm, updation of the tree is divided into four parts.

1. If weight of any edge is increasing and that is not the part of SPT.
2. If weight of any edge is increasing and that is part of SPT.
3. If weight of any edge is decreasing and that is not part of SPT.
4. If weight of any edge is decreasing and that is part of SPT.

All the above given cases may occur one by one or all together. For these mentioned cases we have implemented our algorithm and tested for multiple edge weight changes with all combinations.

Our focus is to just update only affected part of the tree. If we shall do that then the size of tree which is to be updated will de reduced drastically, and it shall reduce time required to compute SPT for new updated graph. If we talk about the time complexity to find SPT then, first time it will take same time as Dijkstra's SPT time, because at that time no SPT is calculated before and it will be calculated according to the Dijkstra's algorithm only. But for the next and so forth when any updation will occur then it shall visit only affected part and give new SPT for that graph.

The question which may arise is why the weight of the edges will increase? The reason is traffic or any other variable factor which changes or may change with time and usage, or it may be the failure of access of that link (edge), because of which one will have to select new path to travel. So the weight of the edges may increase or decrease.

For this type of approach some papers and research works are referred which are discussed in further sections. Some of them algorithms like Ball-and-String model and FMN algorithm are semi-dynamic(either working for increasing or decreasing weights) and some are not correct. Here the proposed algorithm is fully-dynamic algorithm and working with all conditions.

Chapter 2. **Related Theory**

2.1 Introduction

Graph is collection of Edges and Vertices, or we can say set of Edges and Vertices. In which the vertices are connected to each other by edges. In some graphs directions are not specified and these types of graph are known as undirectional graph, and if directions are given then those are known as directional graphs. Direction of the edges denotes that from which vertex to which vertex one can move.

If edges are not having assigned weight then the graph is known as unweighted graph, and if weights are assigned to edges then that graph is known as weighted graph. These weights may be based on the traveling complexity from source node to destination node, and this complexity or factor may be considered depending on the situation. Like if we are representing cities then, cities will be considered as vertices and roads connecting them will be considered as edges, and distance will be considered as weight of that edge. In case of computer networks, routers may be considered as vertices and link between two vertices will be considered as edges, transmission time between two routers may be considered as weight of the vertices.

As explained in the above paragraph, weights could be assigned to edges. If weights are going to be invariant with respect to time then graph is known as static graph. But if weights are subjected to change then graph is known as dynamic graph. There may be different-different factors, which may affect weight of the edges. Like in case of cities graph, traffic condition may be a factor which will vary weights, and in case of computer networks, packet congestion may be the factor which will surely affect the weight of the graph.

But as all know, that world always want to minimize traveling time, whether one has to go from one city to another city, or has to send data packets from one computer to another, or has to do some computation based on graphs. So to achieve goal node, system computes shortest path from source to destination node. But some time system compute shortest path to all nodes from any one source node, then it is known as single source shortest path tree (SPT)

SPT- SPT stands for shortest path tree in which all the nodes are connected to form a tree with minimum cost traversal from source to that node if that is reachable from source node, and no cycle should be formed. Even systems are using some algorithms to find shortest path, most popular one is Dijkstra's SPT algorithm. The main problem with this algorithm is that, it is efficient for static graph only. For dynamic graph where weights are suppose to be changed frequently, algorithm will take same time as it had never calculated SPT before.

Time complexity of Dijkstra's SPT algorithm is $O(n^2)$. For few nodes it's bearable, but for graph having millions of node will make a large effect. And to traverse entire graph even if small part of the graph is affected is not a good approach. So, to improve this, researchers are working to minimize time. Some of them are discussed in literature survey section.

2.2 Proposed Algorithm:-

Here proposed system is dividing the graph in basically two parts one is which is not affected from the weight changes and other is affected. For this following algorithm is used.

In proposed algorithm, updation of the tree is divided into four parts.

1. If weight of any edge is increasing and that is not the part of SPT.
2. If weight of any edge is increasing and that is part of SPT.
3. If weight of any edge is decreasing and that is not part of SPT.
4. If weight of any edge is decreasing and that is part of SPT.

2.3 Dynamic Graph

All the above given cases may occur one by one or all together. For these mentioned cases this proposed system has implemented algorithm and tested for multiple edge weight changes with all combinations.

Proposed algorithm's focus is to just update only affected part of the tree. If system shall do that then the size of tree which is to be updated will be reduced drastically, and it shall reduce time required to compute SPT for new updated graph. If anybody talks about the time complexity to find SPT then, first time, it will take same time as Dijkstra's SPT time, because at that time no SPT is calculated before and it will be calculated according to the Dijkstra's algorithm only. But for the next and so forth when any updation will occur then it shall visit only affected part and give new SPT for that graph.

The question which may arise is why the weight of the edges will increase? The reason is traffic or any other variable factor which changes or may change with time and usage, or it may be the failure of access of that link (edge), because of which one will have to select new path to travel. So the weight of the edges may increase or decrease.

For this type of approach some papers and research works are referred which are discussed in further sections. Some of them algorithms like Ball-and-String model and FMN algorithm are semi-dynamic(either working for increasing or decreasing weights) and some are not correct. Here the proposed algorithm is fully-dynamic algorithm and working with all conditions.

2.4 Used Datastructures and Algorithm

Here concern is to find new SPT whenever there is any change in the existing graph. And these changes may occur in some possibilities. Here in proposed algorithm the problem has been divided in four sub problems.

9

1. Weight of any edge is increasing and that edge is part of existing SPT.
2. Weight of any edge is increasing and that edge is not part of existing SPT.
3. Weight of any edge is decreasing and that edge is part of existing SPT.
4. Weight of any edge is decreasing and that edge is not part of existing SPT.

For all these, case sections are proposed separately, and only affected part of the graph is focused so that time could be minimized.

Variables and data structures which are used in algorithm are as follows:-

- **settledNodes** having set of vertex which are settled.
- **unSettledNodes** having set of vertices which are traversed but not connected to tree yet.
- **nonVisitedNodes** having set of vertices which are never visited and not connected to the graph having source.
- **predecessors** used to store vertices and their predecessor.
- **distance** is used to map distance of that node from source.

2.4.1 Methods used:-

- **removeSettled(Vertex):** this method will be used to remove settled vertex from the settledNodes if that is affected by the weight change.
- **executeAfterChangeD(Vertex, int):** this method will be called when the weight of any edge is decreased and edge is in SPT by passing its destination vertex and difference in weight.
- **executeAfterChangeI(Vertex):** this method will be called when weight of any edge is increasing and that edge is present in SPT.
- **executeAfterChangeDecreaseNotConnected (Vertex):** this method will be called when weight of any edge is decreasing and that edge is not present in SPT.

If weight of any edge is increasing and that edge is not present in SPT then just weight of edge will be updated.

Now we will look into the methods that what actually are they doing.

1. executeAfterChangeD(Vertex source, int diff)

Extract neighbour of that source node and store them in neighbor list

If the predecessor of that neighbor is this source

Then

just update the distance of that node by passed diff value.

Call

executeAfterChangeD(Vertex node, int diff)

Else

If that node is not successor of this source node in SPT

Then

Check the distance of node if it's decreasing

Then

Make that node unsettled. And start calculating SPT for that section

End.

2. executeAfterChangeI(Vertex source)

Make unsettle this source node and calculate its shortest distance

For all successive nodes do the same by calling and pass this current node as source executeAfterChangeI(Vertex source).

3.executeAfterChangeDecreaseNotConnected(Vertex source)

Find all parent node of this source node.

With all parent nodes check it's distance and select minimum one.

Change its predecessor to that parent node.

Now take all successors one by one and update their costs.

Stop.

2.5 EXPERIMENTAL PROOF AND EXAMPLES

2.5.1. Proofs

In experiment one randomly generated graph having given number of nodes and random number of edges is considered. And the SPT of that graph is found by using both the algorithms one which we have proposed and other is well known Dijkstra's algorithm.

Now have a look on all the cases one by one and analysis on time taken by proposed algorithm. Let us say weight of edge from node 0 to node 2 is updated to 2 from 6. Then in this case only encircled part of the tree will be traversed first, their distances from the source node will updated by 4 i.e. the difference in weight. In this case these nodes which are present in successor to that edge will not change their parent since they are already forming SPT and if weight is decreasing in that SPT then it is going to be remain same.

The proof can be given as follows.

Case 1. If weight of any edge is increasing and that is not the part of SPT

As in Figure 2.2 two node are there which are present in SPT with cost c and c*. Here c+w > c* therefore node with cost c* is not attached in success of cost c.

In such case any increment in w will not make any changes in SPTs.

Lemma:- If edge increases its weight from w to w+d then since c+w > c* => c+w+d > c*, no need to scan any node further just update weight of that edge and stop.

Case 2. If weight of any edge is increasing and that is part of SPT.

With the reference of Figure 2.3, nodes n1 and n2 are two nodes present in SPT with different-different sub trees. In this case if cost c increases to c+d then all its successors will get unsettled i.e. need to check all the nodes present in that subtree.

13

Lemma: $c < c^*+w$ and in case if $c+d > c^*+w$ because here d is always positive so it may occur or some where any other successive node it may be and at that time those node will get unsettled will need to be attached to its some other parent nodes having minimum cost.

Case 3. If weight of any edge is decreasing and that is not part of SPT

When weight of that edge decreases which is not present in SPT then in that case node which is successor to that edge is to be checked and if this cost is not less than previous cost of that node then we will just update edge weight and stop there only. And in case if this newly calculated cost is less than previous cost then that node will get unsettled and get its new parent this parent is the origin of that edge. And no need to do any other changes for further successive nodes. But those nodes which are successors of that subtree nodes but not present in that subtree for that SPT, may get attached to them since here it is possible to get other minimum cost path due to decrease in weights in predecessor's edge, so here we will have to check all those nodes also which are successors of those nodes which are present in that SPT subtree.

Lemma: we shall consider situation in Figure 2.1. where n1, n2 and n3 are in same subtree and n2, n5 are in other subtree. It is sure that $c+c^* < c'+w$ that's why that is in other subtree. If weight w decreases by d then it may be the case that $c+c^* > c'+w-d$ and in that case n3 will change its parent node to n2. And n4 is having its minimum cost via n3 i.e. $c+c^*+c''$ is smaller than all other costs which are reachable to n4. Or we can say c'' is already shortest path from n3 and edge from n2 to n3 is not present in SPT but after decreasing its weight it may give minimum cost but this is not going to affect subtree having root n3, so no need to check for its successors.

Now taking case of node n5, assume there is any edge from n4 to n5 with weight w', previously n5 was not present as a successor of n4 in that subtree in which n4 is present but when w reduces by some weight d then it may be the case that $c'+w-d+c''+w' < c'+c'^*$, and n5 will get attached to n4.

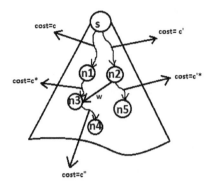

Figure 2.1: Edge from n2 to n3 is not in SPT and weight w decreases its weight by d.

Case 4. If weight of any edge is decreasing and that is part of SPT

If cost of any node from the source is c* and the edge at the destination of which this node is attached decreases its weight by d, then node having cost c* will have now c*-d which is again minimum as shown in figure 2.2.

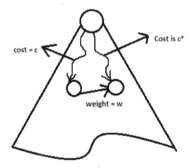

Figure 2.2: SPT having two subtrees with costs c and c* for two distinct nodes.

Before updation of cost=c*. and this is present in SPT i.e. c*< c+w. here c*decreases to c*-d.

c*< c+w => c*-d < c+w . it proves that nodes present in that sub tree will not change their parents, but nodes which are not present in that subtree may get updated minimum cost so they may change their parent as explained and proved in next paragraph.

Here n1 and n2 are two nodes of SPT but having different subtrees.Node n2 is not successor of n1 since c*+w > c, if c* decreases by d then c*-d+w < c may be the case, and in this case n2 will get unsettled and attached to n1 and all its successors will also be shifted and in case if c*-d+w > c then that successor node will remain at same position as it is having.

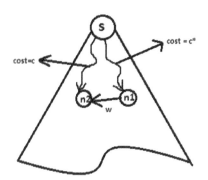

Figure 2.3. SPT having two subtrees with costs c and c* for two distinct nodes n2 and n1 respectively. Node n2 is also successor of n1 with cost w.

2.5.2. Factors Evaluated

- **Graph Size:** This is number of nodes (vertices) and number of edges connecting them.
- **Number of edges updated:** This is number of edges changing its value, either increasing or decreasing.

Chapter 3. **Literature Survey**

3.1 Fully Dynamic Algorithm

Frigioni et al.[1] proposed a fully dynamic algorithm, for finding Shortest Path Tree in the given dynamic graph. In this algorithm each node has to maintain information of its parent node which restrict the number of nodes to be scanned each time when ever weight changes. It follows the same approach as Dijkstra's algorithm does but this is with minimum number of node search. According to author this algorithm is having less theoretical complexity but the data structures used are complex which makes the system inefficient, since its time consuming. This is shown experimentally in [2] by Frigioni that it is performing well.

3.2 BallString

Narváez et al. [3] proposed an algorithm for SPT, where its finding SPT for the given graph and at the same time if any changes in weights occur it re-arranges themselves. And this is having a central idea of Ball and string model where some balls are tied together and any one of these is picked up and automatically all the balls are arranged with SPT i.e. all stretched strings shows travelling path between nodes. If any thread is shortened then all the affected nodes will set itself. In [4] one intelligent approach is proposed to recompute the SPT for the multiple weight changes in any dynamic graph. Here algorithms is called ball-string model since affected nodes are rearranging them in natural way with minimum complexity and in economical way, its really a great idea. This approach reduces unnecessary changes for any update in edges and do not process those parts which is not affected in any case i.e. after evaluating SPT again will give same results for those nodes.

In [5] this is shown that unfortunately this algorithm does not work correctly for multiple weight changes and updates.

3.3 DynamicSWSF-FP

Ramalingam and Reps in [5] propose a fully dynamic algorithm, DynamicSWSF-FP, Where they have given algorithm to update the SPT for any changes in edges. Here tree is used to compute minimum number of steps to derive any terminal strings from one or more non-terminal strings by using production rules. Here a graph is generated which can vary its edge weight. The main approach is given as follows: At any instant, a "right-hand side" (rhs) value, which maintains every vertex in the Graph(G) and denoted as rhs(v). this tracks the shortest distance which v gets by their all parents. dv is the shortest distance information for each vertex v in G, and one equality is represented as dv=rhs(v) before any input edge weight updates. As soon as edge weight is updated, DynamicSWSF-FP updates affected vertices, and it tries to access minimum number of edges and makes it equal to rhs(v) again.

A disadvantage of DynamicSWSF-FP is that it computes the rhs value too often, which leads to a high number of edge visits. In the same paper [6], the authors suggest some improvement on computing rhs values incrementally. The authors maintain a heap for each affected vertex. The improved algorithm is proven to be correct, but too many heaps may not be practical.

Chapter 4. **Design Methodology**

4.1 Flowcharts.

4.1.1 changeWeight

changeWeight is a method, which is called when any edge or group of edges change it weight. Flow of the function calls and algorithm is as follows as shown in figure 4.1.

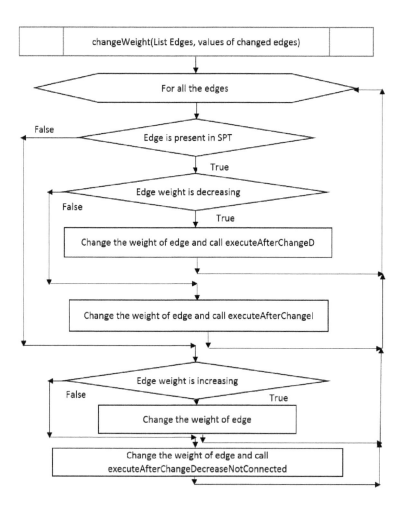

Figure 4.1. Flowchart of changeWeight method

Here in the implementation parameters which are passed to the function are the edges which are changing its weight and new values of those edges. Here implementation has considered all the updates serially.

For all the edges, first condition which is checked is whether that edge is existing in the calculated SPT or not. If that edge is existing then next condition which is checked is whether the weight is increasing or decreasing.

If the edge is existing in the SPT and weight is decreasing then the method executeAfterChangeD is called. This method take care of updation of the SPT for that case, this is case 4 mentioned in section 2.5.1.

And If that edge is existing in the SPT and weight is increasing then the method executeAfterChangeI is called. This method take care of updation of the SPT for this case, which is mentioned in case 2 in section 2.5.1.

If the very first condition itself doesn't satisfy that is edge is not the part of the SPT then it goes for the condition check whether weight is increasing or decreasing. If the weight is increasing then only the weight is updated and no need to call any method for any other updation as mentioned in case 1 in section 2.5.1.

And after not satisfying the condition for not existing in SPT if it is found that the weight is decreasing then the weight of that edge is updated and method executeAfterChangeDecreaseNotConnected is called, this is the implementation of case 3 in section 2.5.1.

4.1.2 executeAfterChangeD

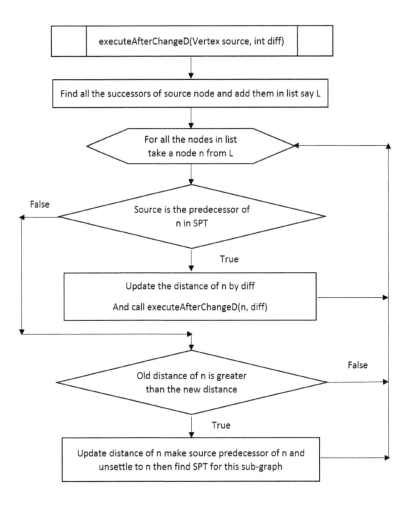

Figure 4.2. Flowchart of executeAfterChangeD method

executeAfterChangeD is a method which is called when the weight of any edge decreases. Two parameters are passed to this method first one is the destination vertex of the edge of which the weight is to be updated and the other is the new weight of that edge.

As shown in the Figure 4.2, when this method is called then all the successor nodes are found out and stacked in to a list so that one by one their distance could be updated, This job is done differently for different cases as mentioned as follows.

If this node is the successor of source node in SPT also then the distance is updated and all the successors of this node would be stacked in list only and recursively an executeAfterChangeD would be called until list gets empty.

If the node is not the successor of source in SPT then new distance will be calculated and if this distance is less than the older one then all the successor nodes of this node present in that SPT would get unsettled and will find their parent node for shortest distance.

If the node is not the successor of source in SPT and new distance is same or greater the previous then nothing will happen and sub-graph from that node will be discarded.

All these steps will be called recursively and repeatedly until list gets empty.

4.1.3 executeAfterChangeI

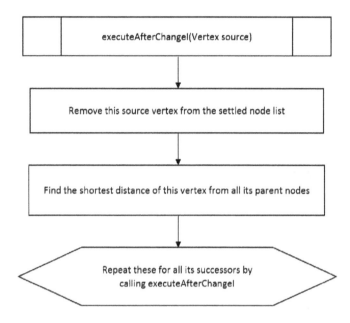

Figure 4.3. Flowchart of executeAfterChangeI method

As shown in figure 4.3 this method is called for that node whose distance is increasing and causing edge is not present in SPT.

The source node is removed from the settled node list and the shortest distance path is computed. Its all other successor nodes will follow the same procedure as its parent did and one by one by calling executeAfterChangeI all the affected nodes would get settled.

4.1.4 DijkstraSPT

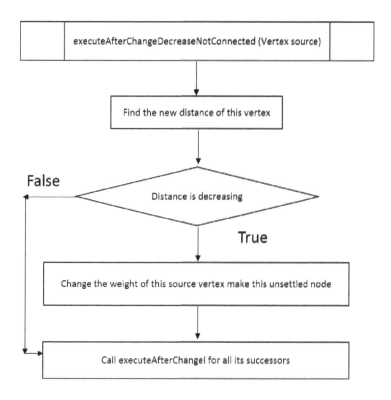

Figure 4.4. Flowchart of executeAfterChangeDecreaseNotConnected method

In Figure 4.4. executeAfterChangeDecreaseNotConnected is called for the destination node of the changing edge. Algorithm will calculate first the distance of this node via changing edge. If distance is decreasing then update distance of the node and call executeAfterChangeI for all its successors. If distance is not increasing then just call executeAfterChangeI for all the successors.

4.1.5 DijkstraSPT

Class DijkstraSPT
private final List<Vertex> nodes; private final List<Edge> edges; private Set<Vertex> settledNodes; private Set<Vertex> unSettledNodes; private Set<Vertex> nonVisitedNodes; private Map<Vertex, Vertex> predecessors; private Map<Vertex, Integer> distance;
public DijkstrasSPT(Graph graph) public void execute(Vertex source, int n) public void execute2(Vertex source, int n) public void removeSettled(Vertex source) public void executeAfterChangeD(Vertex source, int diff) public void executeAfterChangeI(Vertex source) public void executeAfterChangeDecreaseNotConnected(Vertex source) private List<Vertex> findParent(Vertex source) private int getWeight(Vertex s, Vertex v) private void findMinimalDistances(Vertex node) private int getDistance(Vertex node, Vertex target) private List<Vertex> getNeighborsAfter(Vertex node) private List<Vertex> getNeighbors(Vertex node) private Vertex getMinimum(Set<Vertex> vertexes) private boolean isSettled(Vertex vertex) private int getShortestDistance(Vertex destination) public LinkedList<Vertex> getPath(Vertex target) public void changeWeight(List<Edge> chedges, Map<String, Integer> e) public Map getPredecessors()

Figure 4.2. DijkstraSPT class

27

Figure4.2 shows DijkstraSPT class, this is implementing proposed Dynamic algorithm. This figure is showing structure of class DijkstraSPT class with its data members, and member functions. As the name of the method suggest they do their respective jobs.

4.1.6 DijkstraSPT constructor

Figure 4.3 shows the constructor, which takes a graph and initializes its nodes and edges.

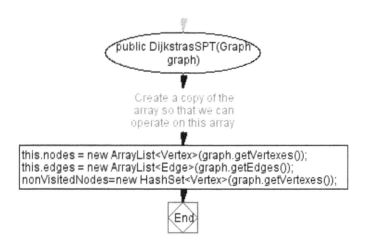

Figure 4.3.

4.1.7 Execute method

Figure 4.4 is showing the flow of code to settle down all the nodes with SPT. This will continue until all the nodes are settled. And this SPT is started with start node , here we are not considering disconnected graph. Only the nodes which are reachable from the source node are considered.

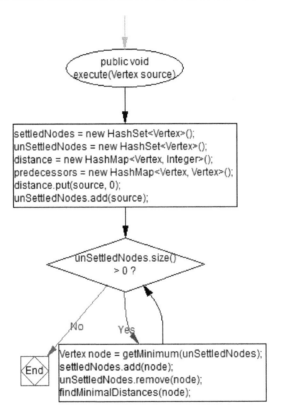

Figure 4.4

4.1.8 getDistance

Figure 4.5 is showing the method to compute the distance of any node from its predecessors which is passed to this method. Where condition 1 is to check whether that particular edge is connecting that node with target or not if yes then weight of that edge is returned.

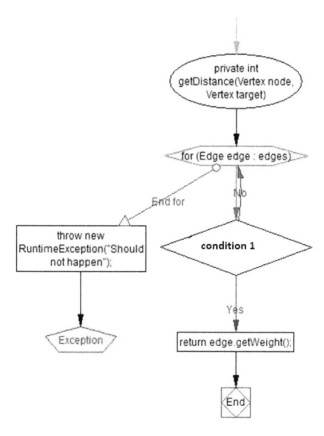

Figure 4.5

4.1.9 findMinimalDistances

Figure 4.6 is showing the logic for finding minimum distance of any node to all its successors . When that successor with the minimum distance is detected, that node will be attached to the SPT with respective predecessor.

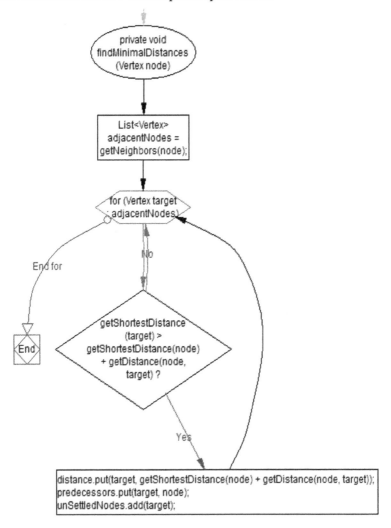

Figure 4.6.

4.1.10 getNeighbors

Figure 4.7 is showing the logic to find all the successive neighbour nodes (which are not settled) of any node.

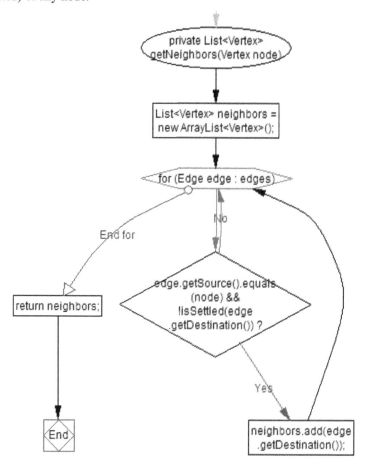

Figure 4.7

4.1.11 getMnimium

In figure 4.8, method is used to find the vertex having minimum distance among all unsettled vertices.

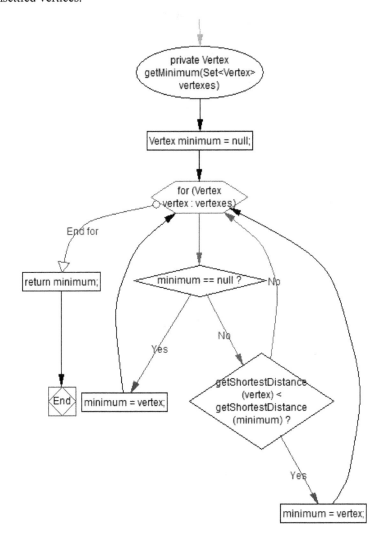

Figure 4.8

4.1.12 isSettled

In figure 4.9 method is used to check whether any node is settled or not, if that is settled then true is returned else false will be returned.

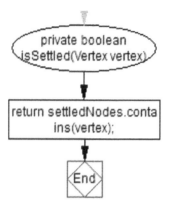

Figure 4.9

4.1.13 getShortestDistance

This method shown in figure 4.10 is used to find the distance of any vertex which is already calculated and mapped to that. If that is not attached then it will get ∞ distance, but here i.e. given as MAX value possible.

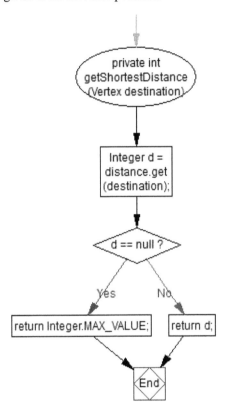

Figure 4.10

4.1.14 getPath

This method shown in 4.11 is used to find the path to any node from the source in SPT. First it starts from destination vertex and move toward source and at the end reverses the order.

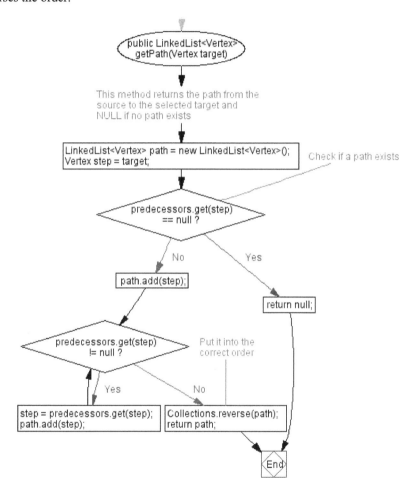

Figure 4.11

4.1.15 changeWeight

Method shown in figure 4.12 is used to update the weights of the edges and to find updated SPT.

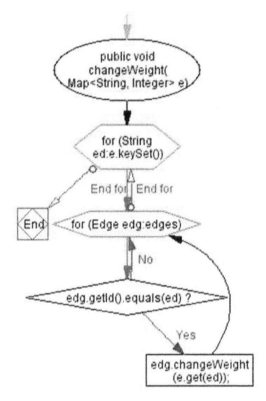

Figure 4.12

Chapter 5. **Results and Discussions**

5.1 Artificial Dataset

Here for analysis work we have used a sample graph as given below. Adjacency matrix can be shown as follows.

	0	1	2	3	4	5	6	7	8	9	10	11	12	13	14	15	16	17	18
0	0	7	6	2															
1	1	0		5		5													
2		5	0						15										
3			14	0	15		13					14							
4					0			8			7								
5						0		6			9								
6		13			12		0		18	12					13				
7								0									16		
8									0	17				3					
9								17	14	0							12		
10					3						0						4		
11												0				9			10
12												8	0			7			
13													2	0	10				
14												10			0		11	11	
15																0			16
16									8					9		7	0		11
17																		0	11
18																		17	0

Table 5.1 Adjacency Matrix

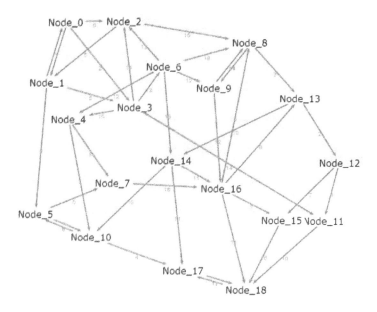

Figure 5.1 Small Graph taken to show correctness and working

5.2 Experimental Results

As per the proposed algorithm here one small sample is taken as shown in Figure4 having 19 vertices and 45 edges and explained its complexity while travelling and updating SPT when any edge or group of edges is updated.

The SPT generated of thes graph shown in figure 5.1 is as shown in Figure 5.2 this is simple Dijkstra's algorithm since initially we have to compute SPT by that only but after this whenever weight will change then SPT is going to be calculated by proposed algorithm. Considering all the cases one by one.

Case 1. If weight of any edge is increasing and that is not the part of SPT

If weight of edge from 4 to 7 changes from 8 to 10which is not in SPT then in this case as discussed in case 1 of section IV. A. no node will be updated or traversed, just algorithm will visit all the edges to find that edge and update its weight, so it may have some time in order of $O(1)$ in best case and $O(E)$ in worst case and average case where E is number of edges present in that graph. And SPT is going to be remain unchanged where as Dijkstra's algorithm will take again O(n2) where n is the number of nodes in that graph.

	Dijkstra's Algorithm	Proposed Algorithm
No.Of vertices visited	$N*N=N^2$	0
No.Of edges visited	E	E
Time complexity	$O(N^2)$ in all cases	$O(1)$ in best case $O(E)$ in average and worst case

Table 5.2 Comparision of Algorithms when weight of any edge is increasing and that is not a part of SPT.

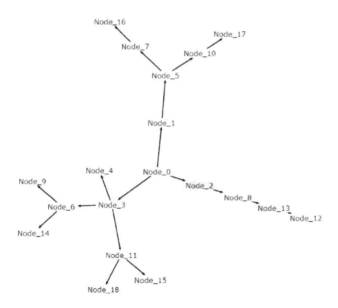

Figure 5.2 SPT for graph in Figure4

41

Case 2. If weight of any edge is increasing and that is the part of SPT

To explain this case if weight of edge from vertex 2 to 8 changes from 15 to 50 then the vertices 8, 13, 12 which are in SPT shown in Figure5 will get unsettled and may need to find their new parents shown in Figure4 , for this process proposed algorithm will visit nodes 2, 6, 9, 16, 8, 13 12 to make them settle down. But to find all these nodes algorithm will need to access all the Edges for 8, 13 and 12 which will take time in order of 3*E i.e. O(E), and time complexity to settle down vertices will be O(db) where d is the depth of that sub-tree and b is the branching factor so complexity would be $O(|E|+|db|)$. To show algorithms correctness updated SPT is shown in Figure 6.

In Graph shown in Figure 4 be updated and total number of nodes traversed are 7, where as in Dijkstra's all 19 vertices will be traversed. Comparison matrix can be shown as follows.

	Dijkstra's Algorithm	Proposed Algorithm
No.Of vertices visited	$N*N=N^2$	bd
No.Of edges visited	E	bd * E
Time complexity	$O(N^2)$ in all cases	O(bd) in best , average and worst case

Table 5.3

In the graph shown in Figure 5.1 which is comparatively very small graph from practical and real life graph. This graph is having limited depth and nodes but in this also it is accessing only 7 out of 19 nodes so only 36.8% of the graph need to be traversed.

Case 3. If weight of any edge is decreasing and that is not part of SPT

If any edge which is not present in SPT let us say from vertex 3 to 2 changes its weight from 14 to 3 then, in first step only vertex 2 is needed to be checked if that is affected then need to change parent of 2 to 3, and rest of the vertex will remain as they are and the cost(distance from the source) of its sub-tree will be updated after that all other nodes will get checked which are successors of node 2, if they get affected then same process will be repeated for their successors also, until we get further successors unchanged. This resultant SPT is shown in Figure 5.3, to find all those vertices which are part of the subtree from that source vertex here in example it is vertex 2, algorithm will have to check all the vertices. There complexity would be O(E+N).

Comparison of proposed algorithm's complexity with Dijkstra's algorithm would be as follows.

	Dijkstra's Algorithm	Proposed Algorithm
No.Of vertices visited	$N*N=N^2$	N
No.Of edges visited	E	E
Time complexity	$O(N^2)$ in all cases	O(E+N) in best , average and worst case

Table 5.4

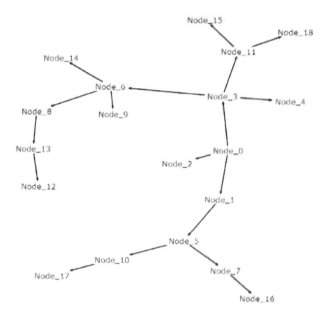

Figure 5.3 SPT after changing weight of edge from vertex 2 to vertex 8 from weight 15 to 50.

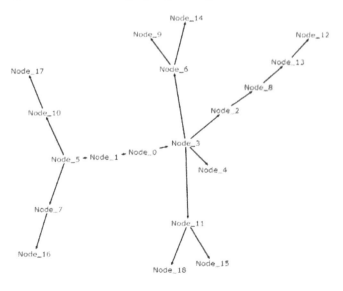

Figure 5.4 SPT after changing weight of edge from vertex 3 to vertex 2 from weight 14 to weight 3.

Case 4. If weight of any edge is decreasing and that is part of SPT.

This case is considered for those edges which are decreasing their weight and they are part of SPT, then proposed algorithm will just update edge weight and distance of vertices present in that sub-tree and halt but the structure of SPT will have same structure. No other changes will be done.

To find sub-tree algorithm will scan all the edges E and only those nodes which are in that sub-tree, so we can say that complexity is O(E).

	Dijkstra's Algorithm	Proposed Algorithm
No.Of vertices visited	$N*N=N^2$	Only subtree
No.Of edges visited	E	E
Time complexity	$O(N^2)$ in all cases	O(E) in best , average and worst case

Table 5.5

Besides implementing our algorithm we have also implemented Dijkstra's SPT algorithm so that we could compare results of our algorithm and Dijkstra's algorithm when we update the graph with multiple edges. In this section we have discussed these results with multiple cases. Here we have generated a graph randomly where we have given number of vertices and edges are generated automatically to generate a Graph having random weights.

X-axis represents number of edges changed, and y-axis represents time taken to find new updated SPT by our proposed algorithm and Dijkstra's algorithm, graph size, number of edges changed and time taken to recomputed SPT by Dijkstra and proposed algorithm are given in figure 5.5 and the graphical comparision is shown in figure 5.6.

45

Graph Size	No. of changed edges	Time by Simple Dijkstra	Proposed Dynamic Algorithm
2000 nodes 5892 edges	1	1903	0
	2	1996	109
	3	1996	46
	4	2137	281
	5	1919	16
	6	2121	249
	7	1519	312
	8	2652	1310
	9	1342	94
	10	1420	156
	20	7301	6053
	30	3510	2262
	100	11731	10390

Figure 5.5. comparative result of Dijkstra's algorithm and proposed algorithm for different number of changed edges.

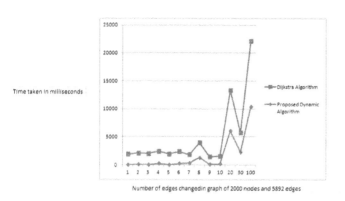

Figure 5.6. Comparative results with 2000 nodes and 5892 edges with mixed weight changes.

In Figure 5.5 the graph which is used is very dense and while changing any edge we get almost constant depth of that SPT tree, so here it might not show a high variation with different number of edges, but where this depth is high this will show a great difference in time.

Chapter 6. **Conclusion, Limitation and Scope for Future Work**

6.1 Conclusions

For Dynamic Shortest Path computation some previous algorithms were already present, however they were static, semi-dynamic or fully dynamic. If they were for fully dynamic then were fail to correctly process multiple edge weights. Proposed algorithm is easy to understand and correctly processes multiple weights. This algorithm works efficiently for changing multiple weights also. If these conditions are given together as an input, then also it is more efficient and computes SPT correctly.

As Compared with Dijkstra's algorithm, this algorithm shows less time complexity in the order of $O(E)$ in most of the cases and in some cases $O(b^d)$ where E is the number of edges present in that graph, d is depth of that affected sub-tree and b is branching factor of the graph, it shows tremendous time reduction for any dense and big network or graph.

Execution of algorithm will show a great change and time reduction if graph will be dense and having high depth. Purpose of this study is to give time efficient algorithm for dynamic graphs where weights of the edges are changing frequently. Algorithm avoids those vertices to traverse which are not likely to be affected with any changes in edge weights. This proposed algorithm gives minimum complexity as compare to Dikstra's algorithm which has been already mentioned in previous topics with analysis.

6.2 Scope for Future Work

Here in this thesis algorithm is proposed for dynamic graph to reduce the complexity. But, the complexity can be further reduced, since this work has considered one directional search with so many recursive calls. If search is conducted bidirectional search method, then in parallel execution complexity will be further reduced.

To perform this bidirectional search one can use heuristic functions and values, these values will be computed in the very first iteration of SPT, and after that the cost of the path will be estimated.

References

[1] D. Frigioni, A. Marchetti-Spaccamela, and U. Nanni, "Fully Dynamic Algorithms for Maintaining Shortest Paths Trees," J. Algorithms, vol. 34, no. 2, pp. 251-281, 2000.

[2] D. Frigioni, M. Ioffreda, U. Nanni, and G. Pasquale, "Experimental Analysis of Dynamic Algorithms for the Single-Source Shortest- Path Problem," ACM J. Experimental Algorithms, vol. 3, p. 5, 1998.

[3] P. Narva'ez, K. Siu, and H. Tzeng, "New Dynamic Algorithms for Shortest Path Tree Computation," ACM Trans. Networking, vol. 8, no. 6, pp. 734-746, 2000.

[4] P. Narva'ez, K. Siu, and H. Tzeng, "New Dynamic SPT Algorithm Based on a Ball-and-String Model," ACM Trans. Networking, vol. 9, no. 6, pp. 706-718, 2001.

[5] Edward P.F. Chan and Yaya Yang,"Shortest Path Tree Computation in Dynamic Graph,"IEEE Transaction On Computers, vol 58. No.4., April 2009.

[6] G. Ramalingam and T.W. Reps, "An Incremental Algorithm for a Generalization of the Shortest-Path Problem," J. Algorithms, vol. 21, no. 2, pp. 267-305, 1996.

[7] E.W. Dijkstra, "A Note on Two Problems in Connection with Graphs," Numerical Math., vol. 1, pp. 269-271, 1959.

[8] B. Xiao, Q. Zhuge, and E.H.M. Sha, "Efficient Algorithms for Dynamic Update of Shortest Path Tree in Networking," J. Computers and Their Applications, vol. 11, no. 1, 2003.

[9] G. Ramalingam and T.W. Reps, "On the Computational Complexity of Dynamic Graph Problems," Theoretical Computer Science, vol. 158, nos. 1-2, pp. 233-277, 1996.

[10] G. Ausiello, G.F. Italiano, A. Marchetti-Spaccamela, and U. Nanni,"Incremental Algorithms for Minimal Length Paths," J. Algorithms, vol. 12, no. 4, pp. 615-638, 1991.

www.ingramcontent.com/pod-product-compliance
Lightning Source LLC
LaVergne TN
LVHW042348060326
832902LV00006B/467